The Poetry of Bliss Carman

Volume XII - Pipes of Pan No II. From the Green Book of the Bards

William Bliss Carman was born in Fredericton, in New Brunswick on April 15th 1861. He was educated at Fredericton Collegiate School before moving to the University of New Brunswick, obtaining his B.A. there in 1881. As is common with so many writers his first published piece was for the University magazine and for Carman that was in 1879.

After several years editing various magazines and periodicals Carman first published a poetry volume in 1893 with Low Tide on Grand Pré. There was no Canadian company prepared to publish and when an American company did so it went bankrupt.

The following year was decidedly better. His partnership with the American poet Richard Hovey had given birth to Songs of Vagabondia. It was an immediate success.

That success prompted the Boston firm, Stone & Kimball, to reissue Low Tide on Grand Pré and to hire Carman as the editor of its literary journal, The Chapbook.

Carman brought out, in 1895, Behind the Arras, a somewhat more serious and philosophical work centered on the premise of a long meditation, using the speaker's house and its many rooms, as a symbol of life and the choices to be made.

In 1896 Carman met Mrs Mary Perry King, who rapidly became patron, adviser and sometime lover. She also became his writing collaborator on two verse dramas.

In 1897 Carman published Ballad of Lost Haven, and in 1898, By the Aurelian Wall, the title poem itself was an elegy to John Keats and the book was a collection of formal elegies.

As the century turned Carman was hard at work on a five-volume set of poetry "Pans Pipes". The excellence of a number of these poems did much to install Carman as the most noted of Canadian Poets and eventually their own Poet Laureate.

In 1912 the final work in the Vagabondia series was published. Richard Hovey had died in 1900 and so this last work was purely Carman's. It has a distinct elegiac tone as if remembering the past works themselves.

On October 28th, 1921 Carman was honored by the newly-formed Canadian Authors' Association where he was crowned Canada's Poet Laureate with a wreath of maple leaves.

William Bliss Carman died of a brain hemorrhage at the age of 68 in New Canaan on the 8th June, 1929.

Index of Contents

TO THE MEMORY OF MY FRIEND

Out of doors are budding trees, calling birds, and opening flowers,
Purple rainy distances, fragrant winds and lengthening hours.

Only in the loving heart, with its unforgetting mind,
There is grief for seasons gone and the friend it cannot find.

For upon this lovely earth mortal sorrow still must bide,
And remembrance still must lurk like a pang in beauty's side.

Ah, one wistful heartache now April with her joy must bring,
And the want of you return always with returning spring!

New York, April, 1903

Lord of my heart's elation,
Spirit of things unseen,
Be thou my aspiration
Consuming and serene!

Bear up, bear out, bear onward
This mortal soul alone,
To selfhood or oblivion,
Incredibly thine own, —

As the foamheads are loosened
And blown along the sea,
Or sink and merge forever
In that which bids them be.

I, too, must climb in wonder,
Uplift at thy command,
Be one with my frail fellows
Beneath wind's strong hand,

A fleet and shadowy column
Of dust or mountain rain,
To walk the earth a moment
And be dissolved again.

Be thou my exaltation
Or fortitude of mien,
Lord of the world's elation
Thou breath of things unseen!

THE GREEN BOOK OF THE BARDS

There is a book not written
By any human hand,
The prophets all have studied,
The priests have always banned.

I read it every morning,
I ponder it by night;
And Death shall overtake me

Trimming my humble light.

He'll say, as did my father
When I was young and small,
"My son, no time for reading!
The night awaits us all."

He'll smile, as did my father
When I was small and young,
That I should be so eager
Over an unknown tongue.

Then I would leave my volume
And willingly obey,
Get me a little slumber
Against another day.

Content that he who taught me
Should bid me sleep awhile,
I would expect the morning
To bring his courtly smile;

New verses to decipher,
New chapters to explore,
While loveliness and wisdom
Grew ever more and more.

For who could ever tire
Of that wild legendry,
The folk-lore of the mountains,
The drama of the sea?

I pore for days together
Over some lost refrain,
The epic of the thunder,
The lyric of the rain.

This was the creed and canon
Of Whitman and Thoreau,
And all the free believers
Who worshipped long ago.

Here Amiel in sadness,
And Burns in pure delight,
Sought for the hidden import
Of man's eternal plight.

No Xenophon nor Caesar

This master had for guide,
Yet here are well recorded
The marches of the tide.

Here are the marks of greatness
Accomplished without noise,
The Elizabethan vigour,
And the Landorian poise;

The sweet Chaucerian temper,
Smiling at all defeats;
The gusty moods of Shelley,
The autumn calms of Keats.

Here were derived the gospels.
Of Emerson and John;
'Twas with this revelation
The face of Moses shone.

Here Blake and Job and Omar
The author's meaning traced;
Here Virgil got his sweetness,
And Arnold his unhaste.

Here Horace learned to question,
And Browning to reply,
When Soul stood up on trial
For her mortality.

And all these lovely spirits
Who read in the great book,
Then went away in silence
With their illumined look,

Left comment, as time furnished
A margin for their skill,
Their guesses at the secret
Whose gist eludes us still.

And still in that green volume,
With ardour and with youth
Undaunted, my companions
Are searching for the truth.

One page, entitled Grand Pré,
Has the idyllic air
That Bion might have envied:
I set a foot-note there.

FIRST CROAK

Northward, crow,
Croak and fly!
Tell her I
Long to go, —

Only am
Satisfied
Where the wide
Maples flame,

Over those
Hills of fir,
Flooding her
Morning snows.

Thou shalt see
Break and sing
Days of spring,
Dawning free.

Northward, crow,
Croak and fly, —
Strive, or die
Striving so!

Darker hearts,
We, than some
Who shall come
When spring starts.

Well I see,
You and I
By and by
Shall get free,

Only now,
Beat away
As we may
Best know how!

Never soar
We, nor float;
But one note,

And no more.

Northward, crow,
Croak and fly!
Would that I
Too might go!

Lark or thrush
Someday, you
Up the blue
Cleave the hush.

O the joy
Then you feel,
Who shall steal
Or destroy?

Have not I
Known how good,
Field and wood,
Stream and sky? —

Longed to free
Soul in flight,
Night by night,
Tree to tree?

Northward, crow,
Croak and fly
You and I, —
Striving, go.

Still though fail
Singing, keep
Croaking deep
Strong and hale!

Flying straight,
Soon we go
Where the snow
Tarries late.

Yet the spring
Is — how sweet!
Hark that beat;
Goldenwing!

Good for all

Faint of heart,
What a start
In his call!

Northward, crow,
Croak and fly,
Though the sky
Thunder No!

A SUPPLICATION

O April, angel of our mortal joy,
Consoler of our human griefs and fears,
Bringer of sunshine to this old grey earth,
Hear once again the prayer of thy lone child,
Return, return!

Mother of solace in the soft spring rain,
Restorer of sane health to wounded souls,
Ah, tarry not thy coming to our doors,
But soon with twilight and the robin's voice,
Return.

Behold, across the borders of the world,
We wait thy reappearance with the flowers,
Disconsolate, dispirited, forlorn,
Our only childish and perpetual prayer,
"Return, return!"

APRIL WEATHER

Soon, ah, soon the April weather
With the sunshine at the door,
And the mellow melting rain-wind
Sweeping from the South once more.

Soon the rosy maples budding,
And the willows putting forth,
Misty crimson and soft yellow
In the valleys of the North.

Soon the hazy purple distance,
Where the cabined heart takes wing,
Eager for the old migration

In the magic of the spring.

Soon, ah, soon the budding windflowers
Through the forest white and frail,
And the odorous wild cherry
Gleaming in her ghostly veil.

Soon about the waking uplands
The hepaticas in blue,
Children of the first warm sunlight
In their sober Quaker hue,

All our shining little sisters
Of the forest and the field,
Lifting up their quiet faces
With the secret half revealed.

Soon across the folding twilight
Of the round earth hushed to hear,
The first robin at his vespers
Calling far, serene and clear.

Soon the waking and the summons,
Starting sap in bole and blade,
And the bubbling, marshy whisper
Seeping up through bog and glade.

Soon the frogs in silver chorus
Through the night, from marsh and swale,
Blowing in their tiny oboes
All the joy that shall not fail,

Passing up the old earth rapture
By a thousand streams and rills,
From the red Virginian valleys
To the blue Canadian hills.

Soon, ah, soon the splendid impulse,
Nomad longing, vagrant whim,
When a man's false angels vanish
And the truth comes back to him.

Soon the majesty, the vision,
And the old unfaltering dream,
Faith to follow, strength to stablish,
Will to venture and to seem;

All the radiance, the glamour,

The expectancy and poise,
Of this ancient life renewing
Its temerities and joys.

Soon the immemorial magic
Of the young Aprilian moon,
And the wonder of thy friendship
In the twilight — soon, ah, soon!

SPRING MAGIC

This morning soft and brooding
In the warm April rain,
The doors of sense are opened
To set me free again.

I pass into the colour
And fragrance of the flowers,
And melt with every bird-cry
To haunt the mist-blue showers,

I thrill in crimson quince-buds
To raptures without name;
And in the yellow tulips
Burn with a pure still flame.

I blend with the soft shadows
Of the young maple leaves,
And mingle in the rain-drops
That shine along the eaves.

I lapse among the grasses
That green the river's brink;
And with the shy wood creatures
Go down at need to drink.

I fade in silver music,
Whose fine unnumbered notes
The frogs and rainy fifers
Blow from their reedy throats.

No glory is too splendid
To house this soul of mine,
No tenement too lowly
To serve it for a shrine.

How is it we inherit
This marvel of new birth,
Sharing the ancient wonder
And miracle of earth?

What wisdom, what enchantment,
What magic of Green Fire,
Could make the dust and water
Obedient to desire?

Keep thou, by some large instinct,
Unwasted, fair, and whole,
The innocence of nature,
The ardour of the soul;

And through the house of being
Thou art at liberty
To pass, enjoy, and linger,
Inviolate and free.

THE ENCHANTRESS

Have you not seen a witch to-day
Go dancing through the misty woods,
Her mad young beauty hid beneath
A tattered gown of crimson buds?

She glinted through the alder swamp,
And loitered by the willow stream,
Then vanished down the wood-road dim,
With bare brown throat and eyes a-dream.

The wild white cherry is her flower,
Her bird the flame-bright oriole;
She comes with freedom and with peace,
And glad temerities of soul.

Her lover is the great Blue Ghost,
Who broods upon the world at noon,
And wooes her wonder to his will
At setting of the frail new moon.

THE MADNESS OF ISHTAR

Vermilion and ashen and azure,
Pigment of leaf and wing,
What will the sorceress Ishtar
Make out of colour and spring?

Of old was she not Aphrodite,
She who is April still,
Mistress of longing and beauty,
The sea, and the Hollow Hill?

Ashtoreth, Tanis, Astarte
A thousand names she has borne,
Since the first new moon's white magic
Was laid on a world forlorn.

Odour of tulip and cherry,
Scent of the apple blow,
Tang of the wild arbutus —
These to her crucible go.

Honey of lilac and willow,
The spoil of the plundering bees,
Savour of sap from the maples —
What will she do with these?

Oboe and flute in the forest,
And pipe in the marshy ground,
And the upland call of the flicker —
What will she make of sound?

Start of the green in the meadow,
Push of the seed in the mould,
Burst of the bud into blossom
What will her cunning unfold?

The waning belt of Orion,
The crescent zone of the moon —
What is the mystic transport
We shall see accomplished soon?

The sun and the rain and the South wind,
With all the treasure they bring —
What will the sorceress Ishtar
Make from the substance of spring?

She will gather the blue and the scarlet,
The yellow and crimson dye,
And weave them into a garment

Of magical texture and ply.

And whoso shall wear that habit
Arid favour of the earth,
He shall be lord of his spirit,
The creatures shall know his worth.

She will gather the broken music,
Fitting it chord by chord,
Till the hearer shall learn the meaning,
As a text that has been restored.

She will gather the fragrance of lilacs,
The scent of the cherry flower,
And he who perceives it shall wonder,
And know, and remember the hour.

She will gather the moonlight and starshine,
And breathe on them with desire,
And they shall be changed on the moment
To the marvel of earth's green fire, —

The ardour that kindles and blights not,
Consumes and does not destroy,
Renewing the world with wonder,
And the hearts of men with joy.

For this is the purpose of Ishtar,
In her great lone house of the sky,
Beholding the work of her hands
As it shall be by and by:

Out of the passion and splendour,
Faith, failure and daring, to bring
The illumined dream of the spirit
To perfection in some far spring.

Therefore, shall we not obey her, —
Awake and be glad and aspire, —
Wise with the ancient knowledge,
Touched with the earthly fire?

In the spell of the wild enchantment
The shy wood creatures know,
Must we not also with Ishtar
Unhindered arise and go?

Hearing the call and the summons,

Heeding the hint and the sign,
Rapt in the flush and the vision,
Shall we demur or repine?

Dare you deny one impulse,
Dare I one joy suppress?
Knowing the might and dominion,
The lure and the loveliness,

Delirium, glamour, bewitchment,
Bidding earth blossom and sing,
Shall we falter or fail to follow
The voice of our mother in spring?

For Love shall be clothed with beauty,
And walk through the world again,
Hearing the haunted cadence
Of an immortal strain;

Caring not whence he wandered,
Fearing not whither he goes,
Great with the fair new freedom
That every earth-child knows;

Impetuous as the wood-wind,
Ingenuous as a flower,
Glad with the fulness of being,
Born of the perfect hour;

Counting not cost nor issue,
Weighing not end and aim,
Sprung' from the clay-built cabin
To powers that have no name.

And with all his soul and body
He shall only seek one thing;
For that is the madness of Ishtar,
Which comes upon earth in springe

A CREATURE CATECHISM

I.

Soul, what art thou in the tribes of the sea?

Lord, said a flying fish,

Below the foundations of storm
We feel the primal wish
Of the earth take form.

Through the dim green water-fire
We see the red sun loom,
And the quake of a new desire
Takes hold on us down in the gloom.

No more can the filmy drift
Nor drafty currents buoy
Our whim to its bent, nor lift
Our heart to the height of its joy.

When sheering down to the Line
Come polar tides from the North,
Thy silver folk of the brine
Must glimmer and forth.

Down in the crumbling mill
Grinding eternally,
We are the type of thy will
To the tribes of the sea.

II.

Soul, what art thou in the tribes of the air?

Lord, said a butterfly,
Out of a creeping thing,
For days in the dust put by,
The spread of a wing

Emerges with pulvil of gold
On a tissue of green and blue,
And there is thy purpose of old
Unspoiled and fashioned anew.

Ephemera, ravellings of sky
And shreds of the Northern light,
We age in a heart-beat and die
Under the eaves of night.

What if the small breath quail,
Or cease at a touch of the frost?
Not a tremor of joy shall fail,
Nor a pulse be lost.

This fluttering life, never still,
Survives to oblivion's despair.
We are the type of thy will
To the tribes of the air.

III.

Soul, what art thou in the tribes of the field?

Lord, said a maple seed,
Though well we are wrapped and b'ound,
We are the first to give heed,
When thy bugles give sound.

We banner thy House of the Hills
With green and vermilion and gold,
When the floor of April thrills
With the myriad stir of the mould,

And her hosts for migration prepare.
We too have the veined twin-wings,
Vans for the journey of air.
With the urge of a thousand springs

Pent for a germ in our side,
We perish of joy, being dumb,
That our race may be and abide
For aeons to come.

When rivulet answers to rill
In snow-blue valleys unsealed,
We are the type of thy will
To the tribes of the field.

IV.

Soul, what art thou in the tribes of the ground?

Lord, when the time is ripe,
Said a frog through the quiet rain,
We take up the silver pipe
For the pageant again.

When the melting wind of the South
Is over meadow and pond,

We draw the breath of thy mouth,
Reviving the ancient bond.

Then must we fife and declare
The unquenchable joy of earth, —
Testify hearts still dare,
Signalise beauty's worth.

Then must we rouse and blow
On the magic reed once more,
Till the glad earth-children know
Not a thing to deplore.

When rises the marshy trill
To the soft spring night's profound,
We are the type of thy will
To the tribes of the ground.

V.

What art thou in the tribes of the earth?

Lord, said an artist born,
We leave the city behind
For the hills of open morn,
For fear of our kind.

Our brother they nailed to a tree
For sedition; they bully and curse
All those whom love makes free.
Yet the very winds disperse

Rapture of birds and brooks,
Colours of sea and cloud,
Beauty not learned of books,
Truth that is never loud.

We model our joy into clay,
Or help it with line and hue,
Or hark for its breath in stray
Wild chords and new.

For to-morrow can only fulfil
Dreams which to-day have birth;
We are the type of thy will
To the tribes of the earth.

SURSUM CORDA

I.

The wind on the sea,
The breath of God over the face of the deep,
Whispers a word
The tribes of his watery dominion rejoice having heard.

To-day through the vaultless chambers
Of the sea, below the range
Of light's great beam to fathom,
Soundless, unsearched of change,

There passed more vague than a shadow
Which is, then is no more,
The aura and draft of being,
Like a breath through an open door.

The myriad fins are moving,
The marvellous flanges play;
Herring and shad and menhaden.
They stir and awake and away.

Ungava, Penobscot, Potomac,
Key Largo and Fundy side,
The droves of the frail sea people
Are arun in the vernal tide.

The old sea hunger to herd them,
The old spring fever to drive,
Within them the thrust of an impulse
To wander and joy and thrive;

Below them the lift of the sea-kale,
Before them the fate that shall be;
As it was when the first white summer
Drew the fog from the face of the sea.

II.

The wind on the hills,
The breath of God over the tops of the trees?
Whispers a word
The tribes of his airy dominion rejoice having heard.

Last night we saw the curtain
Of the red aurora wave,
Through the ungirdered heaven
Built without joist or trave,

Fleeting from silence to silence,
As a mirror is stained by a breath,
The only sign from the Titan
Sleeping in frosty death.

Yet over the world this morning
The old wise trick has been done;
Our legions of rovers and singers,
Arrived and saluting the sun.

The myriad wings atremble,
The marvellous throats astrain,
Come the airy migrant people
In the wake of the purple rain.

One joy that needs no bidding,
One will that does not quail;
The whitethroat up from the barren,
The starling down in the swale;

The honk and clamour of wild geese,
The call of the goldenwing;
From valley to lonely valley,
The long exultation of spring.

III.

The wind on the fields,
The breath of God over the face of the ground,
Whispers a word
The tribes of his leafy dominion rejoice having heard.

Crimson of Indian willow,
Orange of maple plume,
As a web of endless pattern
Falls from a soundless loom,

The wide green marvel of summer
Breaks from catkin and sheath,
So silently only a spirit
Could guess at the spirit beneath.

For these are the moveless people,
Who only abide and endure,
Yet no less feel their heart beat
To the lift of the wild spring lure.

These are the keepers of silence,
Who only adore and are dumb,
With faith's own look of expecting
The bidding they know will come.

The revel of leaves is beginning,
The riot of sap is astir;
Dogwood and peach and magnolia
Have errands they will not defer.

In the long sweet breath of the rainwind,
In the warm, sweet hours of sun,
They arise at the Sursum corda,
A thousand uplifted as one.

IV.

The wind in the street,
The breath of God over the roofs of the town,
Whispers a word
The tribes of the Wandering Shadow rejoice having heard.

The tribes of the Wandering Shadow!
Ah, gypsying spirit of man,
What tent hast thou, what solace,
Since the nomad life began?

Forever, wherever the springtime
Halts by the open door,
The heart-sick are healed in the sunshine,
The sorry are sad no more.

Something brighter than morning
Washes the window pane;
Something wiser than knowledge
Sits by the hearth again.

Within him the sweet disquiet,
Before him the old dismay,
When the hand of Beauty beckons
The wayfarer must away.

"A brother to him who needs me,
A son to her who needs;
Modest and free and gentle;"
This is his creed of creeds.

To-night when the belt of Orion
Hangs in the linden bough,
The girl will meet her lover
Where the quince is crimson now.

For the sun of a thousand winters
Will stop his pendulous swing,
Ere man be a misbeliever
In the scarlet legend of spring.

THE WORD IN THE BEGINNING

In principio erat verbum.

PRELUDE

This is the sound of the Word
From the waters of sleep,
The rain-soft voice that was heard
On the face of the deep,
When the fog was drawn back like a veil, and the sentinel tides
Were given their thresholds to keep.

The South Wind said, "Come forth,"
And the West Wind said, "Go far!"
And the silvery sea-folk heard,
Where their weed tents are,
From the long slow lift of the blue through the Carib keys,
To the thresh on Sable bar.

This is the Word that went by,
Over sun-land and swale,
The long Aprilian cry,
Clear, joyous, and hale,
When the summons went forth to the wild shy broods of the air,
To bid them once more to the trail.

The South Wind said, "Come forth,"
And the West Wind said, "Be swift!"
The fluttering sky-folk heard,

And the warm dark thrift
Of the nomad blood revived, and they gathered for flight,
By column and pair and drift.

This is the sound of the Word
From bud-sheath and blade,
When the reeds and the grasses conferred,
And a gold beam was laid
At the taciturn doors of the forest, where tarried the sun,
For a sign they should not be dismayed.

The South Wind said, "Come forth,"
And the West Wind said, "Be glad!"
The abiding wood-folk heard,
In their new green clad,
Sanguine, mist-silver, and rose, while the sap in their veins
Welled up as of old all unsad.

This is the Word that flew
Over snow-marsh and glen,
When the frost-bound slumberers knew,
In tree-trunk and den,
Their bidding had come, they questioned not whence nor why,
They reckoned not whither nor when.

The South Wind said, "Come forth,"
And the West Wind said, "Be wise!"
The wintering ground-folk heard,
Put the dark from their eyes,
Put the sloth from sinew and thew, to wander and dare,
For ever the old surmise!

This is the Word that came
To the spirit of Man,
And shook his soul like a flame
In the breath of a fan,
Till it burned as a light in his eyes, as a colour that grew
And prospered under the tan.

The South Wind said, Come forth,"
And the West Wind said, "Be free!"
Then he rose and put on the new garb,
And knew he should be
The master of knowledge and joy, though sprung from the tribes
Of the earth and the air and the sea.

I.

THE WORD TO THE WATER PEOPLE

Who hath uttered the formless whisper,
The rumour afloat on the tide,
The need that speaks in the heart,
The craving that will not bide?

For the word without shape is abroad,
The vernal portent of change;
And from winter grounds, empty to-morrow,
The fin-folk will gather and range.

It runs in the purple currents,
Swaying the idle weed;
It creeps by the walls of coral,
Where the keels of the ebb recede;

It calls in the surf above us,
In thunder of reef and key,
And where the green day filters
Through soundless furlongs of sea.

It moves where the moving sea-fans
Shadow the white sea-floor;
It stirs where the dredging sand-runs
Furrow and trench and score.

In channel and cave it finds us,
In the curve of the Windward Isles,
In the sway of the heaving currents,
In the run of the long sea-miles,

In the green Floridian shallows,
By marshes hot and rank,
And below the reach of soundings
Off the Great Bahaman Bank.

The tribes of the water people,
Scarlet and yellow and blue,
Are awake, for the old sea-magic
Is on them to rove anew.

They will ride in the great sea-rivers,
And feed in the warm land streams,
By cliffs where the gulls are nesting,
By capes where the blue berg gleams.

The fleet and shining thousands
Will follow the trackless lead
Of the bidding that rises in them,
The old ancestral need.

Will they mistrust or falter,
Question or turn or veer?
Will they put off their harness of colour,
Or their gaudy hues ungear?

Eager, unwasted, undaunted,
They go and they go. They have heard
The lift of the faint strong summons,
The lure of the watery word.

II.

THE WORD TO THE PEOPLE OF THE AIR

Who hath uttered the wondrous hearsay,
The rumour abroad on the air,
The tribal journey summons,
The signal to flock and fare?

Who hath talked to the shy bird-people,
And counselled the feathered breast
To follow the sagging rain-wind
Over the purple crest?

O tribes of the silver whistle,
And folk of the azure wing,
Who hath revived in a night
The magic tradition of spring?

By shores of the low Gulf Islands,
Where the steaming lands emerge,
By reefs of the Dry Tortugas,
Drenched by the crumbling surge,

From the hot and drowsy shallows
Of the silent Everglades,
From creamy coral beaches
In the breath of the Northeast Trades,

We have heard, without note or warble,
Quaver or chirp or trill,
The far and soft-blown tidings

Summon from hill to hill.

Up from the blue horizon,
By canyon and ridge and plain,
Where ride in misty columns
The spearmen of the rain,

The broods of the light air-people
Will bevy and team and throng,
To fill the April valleys
With gurgle and lisp and song.

They know where the new green leafage
Spreads like the sweep of day,
Over the low Laurentians
And up through the Kootenay.

They know where the nests are waiting,
And the icy ponds are thawed,
For the stir and the sight are on them,
Moving the legions abroad.

The oriole under Monadnoc
Will cast his golden spells;
In deep Ontarian meadows
The reed-bird will loose his bells;

The thrushes will flute over Grand Pré,
The quail by the Manomet shore,
The wild drake feed in the bogan,
The swallow come back to the door.

Tanager, robin, and sparrow,
Grosbeak, warbler and wren,
The children of gladness gather
In clearing and grove and fen

For the bright primeval summer,
In their slumbering heart having heard
A strain of the great Resurgam,
A call of the airy word.

III.

THE WORD TO PEOPLE OF THE WOOD

Who hath uttered the leafy whisper,

The rumour that stirs the bough,
That mounts with the sap, and flushes
The buds with beauty now?

None hath report of the message,
No single authentic word;
Yet the tribes of the wood are stirring
At the tidings they have heard.

To-day will the pear-trees blossom
And the yellow jasmine vines,
Where the soft Gulf winds are surfing
In the dreamy Georgian pines.

To-morrow the peach and the redbud
Will join in the woodland pomp,
Floating their crimson banners
By smoky ridge and swamp;

And the gleaming white magnolias,
In many a city square,
Will unfold in the heavenly leisure
Of the kindly Southern air.

Next day over grey New England
The magic of spring will go,
Touching her marshes with yellow,
Her hills with a purple glow.

Then the maple buds will break
In an orange mist once more,
Through lone Canadian valleys,
From Baranov to Bras d'Or.

And where the snowdrifts vanish
From the floor of their piney home,
Hepatica and arbutus,
The shy wood-children, will come.

The elms on the meadow islands
Will shadow the rustling sedge,
The orchards reveal the glory
Of earth by dike and ledge;

The birch will unsheathe her tassels,
The willow her silver plume,
When the green hosts encamp
By lake and river and flume.

For the tides of joy are running
North with the sap and the sun,
And the tribes of the wood are arrayed
In their splendour one by one.

Not one unprepared nor reluctant,
With ardour unspent they have heard
A note of the woodland music,
A breath of the wilding word.

IV.

THE WORD TO THE PEOPLE OF THE GROUND

Who hath uttered the faint earth-whisper,
The rumour that spreads over ground,
The sign that is hardly a signal,
The sense that is scarcely sound?

Yet listen, the earth is awake,
The magic of April is here;
The all but unobserved signal
Is answered from far and near.

Go forth in the morning and listen,
For the coming of life is good;
The lapsing of ice in the rivers,
The lisping of snow in the wood,

The murmur of streams in the mountains,
The babble of brooks in the hills,
And the sap of gladness running
To waste from a thousand stills.

Go forth in the noonday and listen;
A soft multitudinous stir
Betrays the new life that is moving
In the houses of oak and fir.

A red squirrel chirps in the balsam;
A fox barks down in the clove;
The bear comes out of his tree-bole
To sun himself, rummage and rove.

In the depth of his wilderness fastness
The beaver comes forth from his mound,

And the tiny creatures awake
From their long winter sleep under ground.

Go forth in the twilight and listen
To that music fine and thin,
When the myriad marshy pipers
Of the April night begin.

Through reed-bed and swamp and shallow
The heart of the earth grows bold,
And the spheres in their golden singing
Are answered on flutes of gold.

One by one, down in the meadow,
Or up by the river shore,
The frail green throats are unstopped,
And inflated with joy once more.

O heart, canst thou hear and hearken,
Yet never an answer bring,
When thy brothers, the frogs in the valley,
Go mad with the burden of spring?

So the old ardours of April
Revive in her creatures to-day
The knowledge that does not falter,
The longing that will not stay,

And the love that abides. Undoubting,
In the deeps of their ken they have heard
The ancient unwritten decretal,
The lift of the buoyant word.

FROM AN OLD RITUAL

O dwellers in the dust, arise,
My little brothers of the field,
And put the sleep out of your eyes!
Your death-doom is repealed.

Lift all your golden faces now,
You dandelions in the ground!
You quince and thorn and apple bough,
Your foreheads are unbound.

O dwellers in the frost, awake,

My little brothers of the mould!
It is the time to forth and slake
Your being as of old.

You frogs and newts and creatures small
In the pervading urge of spring,
Who taught you in the dreary fall
To guess so glad a thing?

From every swale your watery notes,
Piercing the rainy cedar lands,
Proclaim your tiny silver throats
Are loosened of their bands.

O dwellers in the desperate dark,
My brothers of the mortal birth,
Is there no whisper bids you mark
The Easter of the earth?

Let the great flood of spring's return
Float every fear away, and know
We are all fellows of the fern
And children of the snow.

FELLOW TRAVELLERS

Green are the buds of the snowball,
And green are the little birds
That come to fill my branches
Full of their gentle words.

What is it, tiny brothers?
What are you trying to say
Over and over and over,
In your broken-hearted way?

Have you, too, darkling rumours
In your sweet vagrancy,
News of a vast encounter
Of storm and night and sea?

THE FIELD BY THE SEA

On a grey day by the sea,

I looked from the window and saw
The beautiful companies of the daisies bow
And toss in the gusty flaw.

For the wind was in from sea;
The heavy scuds ran low;
And all the makers of holiday were abashed,
Caught in the easterly blow.

My heart, too, is a field,
Peopled with shining forms,
Beautiful as the companies of the grass,
And herded by swift grey storms.

A thousand shapes of joy,
Sunlit and fair and wild,
All the bright dreams that make the heart of a man
As the heart of a little child,

They dance to the rune of the world,
The star-trodden ageless rune,
Glad as the wind-blown multitudes of the grass,
White as the daisies in June.

But over them, ah, what storms,
In from the unknown sea,
The uncharted and ever-sounding desolate main
We have called Eternity!

They shudder and quake and are torn,
As the stormy moods race by.
And then in the teeth of remorse, the tempestuous lull,
Once more the hardy cry:

"Fear not, little folk of my heart,
Nor let the great hope in you fail!
Being children of light, ye are made as the flowers of the grass,
To endure and survive ana prevail."

THE DANCERS OF THE FIELD

The wind went combing through the grass,
The tall white daisies rocked and bowed;
Such ecstasy as never was
Possessed the shining multitude.

They turned their faces to the sun,
And danced the radiant morn away;
Of all his brave eye looked upon,
His daughters of delight were they.

And when the round and yellow moon,
Like a pale petal of the dusk
Blown loose above the sea-rim shone,
They gave me no more need to ask

How immortality is named;
For I remembered like a dream
How ages since my spirit flamed
To wear their guise and dance with them.

THE BREATH OF THE REED

I heard the rushes in the twilight,
I overheard them at the dusk of day.

Make me thy priest, O Mother,
And prophet of thy mood,
With ail the forest wonder
Enraptured and imbued.

Be mine but to interpret,
Follow nor misemploy,
The doubtful books of silence,
The alphabet of joy.

A pipe beneath thy fingers,
Blown by thy lips in spring
With the old madness, urging
Shy foot and furtive wing,

A reed wherein the life-note
Is fluted clear and high,
Immortal and unmeasured,
No more than this am I.

Delirious and plangent,
I quiver to thy breath;
Thy fingers keep the notches
From discord and from death.

Unfaltering, unflagging,

Comes the long, wild refrain,
With ardours of the April
In woodnotes of the rain.

Be mine the merest inkling
Of what the shore larks mean,
And what the gulls are crying
The wind whereon they lean.

Teach me to close the cadence
Of one brown forest bird,
Who opens so supremely,
Then falters for thy word.

One hermit thrush entrancing
The solitude with sound,
Give me the golden gladness
Of music so profound.

So leisurely and orbic,
Serene and undismayed,
He runs the measure over,
Perfection still delayed.

No hurry nor annoyance;
Enough for him, to try
The large few notes of prelude
Which put completion by.

In ages long hereafter
His heritor may learn
What meant those pregnant pauses,
And that unfinished turn.

So one shall read thy world-runes
To find them all one day
Parts of a single motive,
Scored in an ancient way.

Till then, be mine to master
One phrase in all that strain,
The dominance of beauty,
The transiency of pain,

As swayed by tides of dreaming,
Or bowed by gusts of thought,
A reed within the river,
I waver and am naught.

POPPIES

I who walk among the poppies
In the burning hour of noon,
Brother to their scarlet beauty,
Feel their fervour and their swoon.

In this little wayside garden,
Under the sheer tent of blue,
The dark kindred in forgetting,
We are of one dust and dew.

They, the summer-loving gipsies,
Who frequent the Northern year;
From an older land than Egypt,
I, too, but a nomad here.

All day long the purple mountains,
Those mysterious conjurors,
Send, in silent premonition,
Their still shadows by our doors.

And we listen through the silence
For a far-off sound, which seems
Like the long reverberant echo
Of a sea-shell blown in dreams.

Is it the foreboded summons
From the fabled Towers of Sleep,
Bidding home the wandered children
From the shore of the great deep?

All day long the sun-filled valley,
Teeming with its ghostly thought,
Glad in the mere lapse of being,
Muses and is not distraught.

Then suffused with earth's contentment,
The slow patience of the sun,
As our heads are bowed to slumber
In the shadows one by one,

Sweet and passionless, the starlight
Talks to us of things to be;
And we stir a little, shaken

In the cool breath of the sea.

COMPENSATION

Not a word from the poplar-tree here on the hill?
Not a word from the stream in the bight of the clove?
Not a word from trail, clearing, or forest, to tell
Their brother returned, how all winter they throve?

The old mountain ledges lay purple in June;
The green mountain walls arose hazy and dark;
I saw, heard, and loved all their beauty anew,
But the soul in my body lay deaf, blind, and stark.

"O, Mother Natura, whom most with full heart,
Boy, stripling, and man, I have loved, dost thou leave
Unanswered thy suppliant, troubled thy son, —
To longing no respite, to doom no reprieve?"

Days, weeks, and months passed. Not a whisper outbroke,
Not a word to be caught, not a hint to be had,
By the soul from the world there, all leisure and sun
In perfection of summer, warm, waiting, and glad!

The rose-breasted grosbeak his triumph proclaimed;
The veery his wildest enchantment renewed;
And yet the old ardours not once were relit,
Nor the heart as of old with wild magic imbued.

Until on an evening unlocked for, "O Son," —
Said the stream in the clove, spoke the wind on the hill?
Did a bird in his sleep find the lost ancient tongue,
Universal and clear, with the shadowy thrill

Mere language has never yet uttered? — "O Son,
Was thy heart cold with doubt, hesitation, dismay,
Or hot with resentment, because, as it seemed,
For awhile it must journey alone and away?

"All winter the torrent must sleep under snow;
All winter ash, poplar, and beech must endure;
All winter thy rapturous brothers, the birds,
Must be silent. Are they, then, downcast or unsure?

"Nay, I but give them their seasons and times,
Their moments of joy and their measure of rest;

They keep the great rhythm of life's come and go
The unwearied repose, the unhurrying zest.

"With April I lifted them, bade longings be;
With June I have plenished their heart to the brim.
Will they question when over the world I have spread
The scarlet of autumn with frost at the rim?

"Behold, while vexation was filling thy days,
Thy deeper self, resting unmindful of harms,
(With who- knows what dreams of the splendid and true
To be compassed at length!) lay asleep in my arms."

The moonlight, mysterious, stately, and blue,
Lay out on the great mountain wall, deep and still;
Far below the stream talked to itself in the clove;
The poplar-tree talked to itself on the hill.

THE SPELL

I hung a string of verses
Against my cabin wall.
What think you was the fortune
They prayed might me befall?

Not fame nor health nor riches
To tarry at my door,
But that my vanished sweetheart
Might visit me once more.

Out of the moted day-dream
Among the boding firs,
They prayed she might remember
The lover that was hers.

They prayed the gates of silence
A moment might unclose,
The hour before the hill-crest
Is flushed with solemn rose.

O prayers of mortal longing,
What latch can ye undo?
What comrade once departed
Ever returned for you?

All day with tranquil spirit

I kept my cabin door,
In wonder at the beauties
I had not seen before.

I slept the dreamless slumber
Of happiness again;
And when I woke, the thrushes
Were singing in the rain.

A FOREST SHRINE

When you hear that mellow whistle
In the beeches unespied,
Footfall soft as down of thistle
Turn aside!

That's our golden hermit singer
In his leafy house and dim,
Where God's utterances linger
Yet for him.

Built out of the firmamental
Shafts of rain and beams of sun,
Norse and Greek and Oriental
Here are one.

Gothic oak and Latin laurel
Here but sentry that wild gush
Of wood-music with their aural
Calm and hush.

From those hanging airy arches
Soars the azure roof of June,
While among the feathery larches
Hangs the moon.

Through that unfrequented portal,
When the twilight winds are low,
Messengers of things immortal
Come and go;

Whispers of a rumour hidden
From slow reason, and revealed
To the child of beauty bidden
Far afield;

Hints of rapture rare and splendid
Furnished to the heart of man,
As if, where mind's journey ended,
Soul's began;

As if, when we sighed, "No farther!
Here our knowledge pales and thins;"
One had answered us, "Say rather,
'Here begins.'"

Argue me, "There is no gateway
In this great wall we explore,"
Till there comes a bird-note; straight-way,
There's the door!

Enter here, thou beauty-lover,
The domain where soul resides;
Ingress thought could not discover,
Sense provides.

Ponder long and build at leisure,
Architect; yet canst thou rear
Such a house for such a treasure
As is here?

Leader of the woods and brasses,
Master of the winds and strings,
Hast thou music that surpasses
His who sings?

You who lay cold proof's embargos
On all wonder-working, tell
Whence those fine reverberant largos
Sink and swell!

Hark, that note of limpid glory
Melts into the old earth-strain,
And begins the woodland story
Once again.

Hark that transport of contentment
Blown into a mellow reed,
Wild, yet tranquil soul's preventment
Of soul's need.

There the master voluntaries
On his pipe of greenish gold;
The wise theme whereon he varies,

Never old.

What do we with those who grieve them
O'er the fevers of the mind?
Beauty's follower will leave them
Far behind.

As the wind among the rushes,
Were it not enough to know
The sure joyance of the thrushes?
Even so.

AMONG THE ASPENS

I.

THE LOST WORD

The word of the wind to the aspens
I listened all day to hear;
But over the hill or down in the swale
He vanished as I drew near.

I asked of the quaking shadows,
I questioned the shy green bird;
But the falling river bore away
The secret I would have heard.

Then I turned to my forest cabin
In a clove of the Kaaterskill;
And at dead of night, when the fire was low,
The whisper came to my sill.

Now I know there will haunt me ever
That word of the ancient tongue,
Whose golden meaning, half divined,
Was lost when the world was young.

I know I must seek and seek it,
Through the wide green earth and round,
Though I come in ignorance at last
To the place of the Grassy Mound.

Yet it maybe I shall find it,
If I keep the patience mild,
The pliant faith, the eager mind,

And the heart of a little child.

II.

LEAF TO LEAF

You know how aspens whisper
Without a breath of air!
I overheard one lisper
Yesterday declare,

"When all the woods are sappy
And the sweet winds arrive,
My dancing leaves are happy
Just to be alive."

And presently another,
With that laconic stir
We take to be each other,
Spoke and answered her,

When the great frosts shall splinter
Our brothers oak and pine,
In the long night of winter
Glad fortitude be thine!"

And where the quiet river
Runs by the quiet hill,
I heard the aspens shiver,
Though all the air was still,

III.

THE PASSER BY

Said Aspen Heart to Quaking Leaf,
"Who goes by on the hill,
That you should tremble at dead of noon
When the whole earth is still?"

Said Quaking Leaf to Aspen Heart,
"A loneliness drew nigh,
And fear was on us, when we heard
The mountain rain go by."

Said Aspen Heart to Quaking Leaf,

"Who went by on the hill?
The rain was but your old grey nurse
Crossing the granite sill."

Said Quaking Leaf to Aspen Heart,
"There was a ghostly sigh,
And frosty hands were laid on us,
As the lone fog went by."

Said Aspen Heart to Quaking Leaf,
"But who went by on the hill?
The white fogs were your playfellows,
And your companions still."

Said Quaking Leaf to Aspen Heart,
"We shook, I know not why,
Huddled together when we saw
A passing soul go by."

IV.

THE QUESTION

I wondered who
Kept pace with me, as I wandered through
The mountain gorges blue.

I said to the aspen leaves,
The timorous garrulous tribe of the forest folk,
"Who people the wilderness,
When the wind is away,
And sparrow and jay
Keep silence of noon on a summer day?"
And the leaves replied,
"You must question our brother the rain of the mountain-side."

Then I said to the rain,
The fleeing silvery multitudes of the rain,
"Who people the wilderness,
When the noon is still,
And valley and hill
Feel their pulses slow to the summer's will?"
And the rain replied,
"You must ask our brother the fog on the outward tide."

Then I said to the fog,
The ancient taciturn companies of the sea-mist,

"Who people the loneliness
When your hordes emerge
On the grey sea verge,
And the wind begins his wailing dirge?"
And the fog replied,
"Inquire of that inquisitor at your side."

Then I asked myself. But he knew,
If report of sense be true,
No more than you.

V.

A SENTRY

All summer my companion
Was a white aspen-tree,
Far up the sheer blue canyon,
A glad door-ward for me.

There at the cabin entry,
Where beauty went and came,
Abode that quiet sentry,
Who knew the winds by name.

And when to that lone portal,
All the clear starlight through,
Came news of things immortal
No mortal ever knew,

That vigilant un weary
Kept solitary post,
And heard the woodpipes eery
Of a fantastic host,

Play down the wind in sadness,
Play up the wind in glee,—
The ancient lyric madness,
The joy that is to be.

They passed; the music ended;
And through those rustling leaves
The morning sun descended,
With peace about my eaves.

THE GREEN DANCERS

When the Green Dance of summer
Goes up the mountain clove,
There is another dancer
Who follows it for love.

To the sound of falling water,
Processional and slow
The children of the forest
With waving branches go;

And to the wilding music
Of winds that loiter by,
By trail, ravine and stream-bed.
Troop up against the sky.

The bending yellow birches,
The beeches cool and tall,
Slim ash and flowering locust,
My gipsy knows them all.

And light of foot she follows,
And light of heart gives heed,
Where in the blue-green chasm
The wraiths of mist are freed.

For when the young winged maples
Hang out their rosy pods,
She knows it is a message
From the primeval gods.

When tanager and cherry
Show scarlet in the sun,
She slips her careworn habit
To put their gladness on.

And where the chestnuts flower
Along the mountain-side,
She, too, assumes the vesture
And beauty of their pride.

She hears the freshening music
That ushers in their day,
When from the hemlock shadows
The silver thrushes play.

When the blue moth at noonday

Lies breathing with his wings,
She knows what piercing woodnote
Across the silence rings.

And when the winds of twilight
Flute up the ides of June,
Where Kaaterskill goes plainward
Under a virgin moon,

My wild mysterious spirit
For joy cannot be still,
But with the woodland dancers
Must worship as they will.

From rocky ledge to summit
Where lead the dark-tressed firs,
Under the open starshine
Their festival is hers.

She sees the moonlit laurel
Spread through the misty gloom
(The soul of the wild forest
Veiled in a mesh of bloom).

Then to the lulling murmur
Of leaves she, too, will rest,
Curtained by northern streamers
Upon some dark hill-crest.

And still, in glad procession
And solemn bright array,
A dance of gold-green shadows
About her sleep will play ;

Her signal from the frontier,
There is no bar nor toll
Nor dearth of joy forever
To stay the gipsy soul.

THE WIND AT THE DOOR

Often to my open door
Comes a twilight visitor.

When the mountain summer day
From our valley takes his way,

And the journeying shadows stride
Over the green mountain-side,

Down the clove among the trees
Moves the ghostly wandering breeze.

With the first stars on the crest
And the pale light in the west,

He comes up the dark ravine
Where no traveller is seen.

Yet his coming makes a stir
In the house of Ash and Fir:

"Master, is't in our abode
You will tarry on the road?"

"Nay, I like your roof-tree well,
But with you I may not dwell."

Birches whisper at their sill,
As he passes up the hill:

"Stranger, underneath our boughs
There is ample room to house."

"Friends, I have another quest
Than your cool abiding rest."

And the fluttering Aspen knows
Whose step by her doorway goes:

"Honour, Lord, thy silver tree
And the chamber laid for thee."

"Nay, I must be faring on,
For to-night I seek my own.

"Breath of the red dust is he
And a wayfarer like me;

"Here a moment and then lost
On a trail confused and crossed.

"And I gently would surprise
Recognition in his eyes;

"Touch his hand and talk with him
When the forest light is dim,

"Taking counsel with the lord
Of the utterable word."

Hark, did you hear some one try
The west window furtively,

And then move among the leaves
In the shadow of the eaves?

The reed curtain at the door
Rustled; there's my visitor

Who comes searching for his kin.
"Enter, brother; I'm within."

AT THE YELLOW OF THE LEAF

The falling leaf is at the door;
The autumn wind is on the hill;
Footsteps I have heard before
Loiter at my cabin sill.

Full of crimson and of gold
Is the morning in the leaves;
And a stillness pure and cold
Hangs about the frosty eaves.

The mysterious autumn haze
Steals across the blue ravine,
Like an Indian ghost that strays
Through his olden lost demesne.

Now the goldenrod invades
Every clearing in the hills;
The dry glow of August fades,
And the lonely cricket shrills.

Yes, by every trace and sign
The good roving days are here.
Mountain peak and river line
Float the scarlet of the year.

Lovelier than ever now
Is the world I love so well.
Running water, waving bough,
And the bright wind's magic spell

Rouse the taint of migrant blood
With the fever of the road,
Impulse older than the flood
Lurking in its last abode.

Did I once pursue your way,
Little brothers of the air,
Following the vernal ray?
Did I learn my roving there?

Was it on your long spring rides,
Little brothers of the sea,
In the dim and peopled tides,
That I learned this vagrancy?

Now the yellow of the leaf
Bids away by hill and plain,
I shall say good-bye to grief,
Wayfellow with joy again.

The glamour of the open door
Is on me, and I would be gone,
Speak with truth or speak no more,
House with beauty or with none.

Great and splendid, near and far,
Lies the province of desire;
Love the only silver star
Its discoverers require.

I shall lack nor tent nor food,
Nor companion in the way,
For the kindly solitude
Will provide for me to-day.

Few enough have been my needs;
Fewer now they are to be;
Where the faintest follow leads,
There is heart's content for me.

Leave the bread upon the board;
Leave the book beside the chair;
With the murmur of the ford,

Light of spirit I shall fare.

Leave the latch-string in the door,
And the pile of logs to burn;
Others may be here before
I have leisure to return.

THE SILENT WAYFELLOW

To-day when the birches are yellow,
And red is the wayfaring tree,
Sit down in the sun, my soul,
And talk of yourself to me!

Here where the old blue rocks
Bask in the forest shine,
Dappled with shade and lost
In their reverie divine.

How goodly and sage they!
Priests of the taciturn smile
Rebuking our babble and haste,
Yet loving us all the while.

In the asters the wild gold bees
Make a warm busy drone,
Where our Mother at Autumn's door
Sits warming her through to the bone.

The filmy gossamer threads
Are hung from the black fir bough,
Changing from purple to green
The half-shut eye knows how.

What is your afterthought
When a red leaf rustles down,
Or the chickadees from the hush
Challenge a brief renown?

When silence falls again
Asleep on hillside and crest,
Resuming her ancient mood,
Do you still say, "Life is best?"

Was this reticence of yours
By the terms of being imposed?

One would say that you dwelt
With shutters always closed.

We have been friends so long,
And yet not a single word
Of yourself, your kith or kin
Or home, have I ever heard.

Nightly we sup and part,
Daily you come to my door;
Strange we should be such mates,
Yet never have talked before.

A cousin to downy-feather,
And brother to shining-fin,
Am I, of the breed of earth,
And yet of an alien kin,

Made from the dust of the road
And a measure of silver rain,
To follow you brave and glad,
Unmindful of plaudit or pain.

Dear to the mighty heart,
Born of her finest mood,
Great with the impulse of joy,
With the rapture of life imbued,

Radiant moments are yours,
Glimmerings over the verge
Of a country where one day
Our forest trail shall emerge.

When the road winds under a ledge,
You keep the trudging pace,
Till it mounts a shoulder of hill
To the open sun and space.

Ah, then you dance and go,
Illumined spirit again,
Child of the foreign tongue
And the dark wilding strain!

In these October days
Have you glimpses hid from me
Of old-time splendid state
In a kingdom by the sea?

Is it for that you smile,
Indifferent to fate and fame,
Enduring this nomad life
Contented without a name?

Through the long winter dark,
When slumber is at my sill,
Will you leave me dreamfast there,
For your journey over the hill?

To-night when the forest trees
Gleam in the frosty air,
And over the roofs of men
Stillness is everywhere,

By the cold hunter's moon
What trail will you take alone,
Through the white realms of sleep
To your native land unknown?

Here while the birches are yellow,
And red is the wayfaring tree,
Sit down in the sun, my soul,
And talk of yourself to me.

PICTOR IGNOTUS

He is a silent second self
Who travels with me in the road;
I share his lean-to in the hills,
He shares my modest town abode.

Under the roof-tree of the world
We keep the gipsy calendar,
As the revolving seasons rise
Above the tree-tops, star by star.

We watch the arctic days burn down
Upon the hearthstone of the sun,
And on the frozen river floors
The whispering snows awake and run,

Then in the still, portentous cold
Of a blue twilight, deep and large,
We see the northern bonfires lit
Along the world's abysmal marge.

He watches, with a love untired,
The white sea-combers race to shore
Below the mossers' purple huts,
When April goes from door to door.

He haunts the mountain trails that wind
To sudden outlooks from grey crags,
When marches up the blue ravine
September with her crimson flags.

The wonder of an ancient awe
Takes hold upon him when he sees
In the cold autumn dusk arise
Orion and the Pleiades;

Or when along the southern rim
Of the mysterious summer night
He marks, above the sleeping world,
Antares with his scarlet light.

The creamy shadow-fretted streets
Of some small Caribbean town,
Where through the soft wash of the trades
The brassy tropic moon looks down;

The palm-trees whispering to the blue
That surfs along the coral key;
The brilliant shining droves that fleet
Through the bright gardens of the sea.

The crimson-boled Floridian pines
Glaring in sunset, where they stand
Lifting their sparse, monotonous lines
Out of the pink and purple sand;

The racing Fundy tides that brim
The level dikes; the orchards there;
And the slow cattle moving through
That marvellous Acadian air;

The city of the flowery squares,
With the Potomac by her door;
The monument that takes the light
Of evening by the river shore;

The city of the Gothic arch,
That overlooks a wide green plain

From her grey churches, and beholds
The silver ribbon of the Seine;

The Indian in his birch canoe,
The flower-seller in Cheapside;
Wherever in the wide round world
The Likeness and the Word abide;

He scans and loves the human book,
With that reserved and tranquil eye
That watched among the autumn hills
The golden leisured pomp go by.

What wonder, since with lavish hand
Kind earth has given him her all
Of love and beauty, he should be
A smiling, thriftless prodigal!

EPHEMERON

Ah, brother, it is bitter cold in here
This time of year!
December is a sorry month indeed
For your frail August breed.

I find you numb this morning on the pane,
Searching in vain
A little warmth to thaw those airy vans,
Arrested in their plans.

I breathe on you; and lo, with lurking might
Those members slight
Revive and stir; the little human breath
Dissolves their frosty death.

You trim those quick antennae as of old,
Forget the cold,
And spread those stiffened sails once more to dare
The elemental air.

Does that thin deep, unmarinered and blue,
Come back to you,
Dreaming of ports whose bearing you have lost,
Where cruised no pirate frost?

Ah, shipmate, there'll be two of us some night,

In ghostly plight,
In cheerless latitudes beyond renown,
When the long frost shuts down.

What if that day, in unexpected guise,
Strong, kind, and wise,
Above me should the great Befriender bow,
As I above you now,

Reset the ruined time-lock of the heart,
And bid it start,
And every frost-bound joint and valve restore
To supple play once more!

THE HERETIC

One day as I sat and suffered
A long discourse upon sin,
At the door of my heart I listened,
And heard this speech within.

One whisper of the Holy Ghost
Outweighs for me a thousand tomes;
And I must heed that private word,
Not Plato's, Swedenborg's, nor Rome's

The voice of beauty and of power
Which came to the beloved John,
In age upon his lonely isle,
That voice I will obey, or none.

Let not tradition fill my ears
With prate of evil and of good,
Nor superstition cloak my sight
Of beauty with a bigot's hood.

Give me the freedom of the earth,
The leisure of the light and air,
That this enduring soul some part
Of their serenity may share!

The word that lifts the purple shaft
Of crocus and of hyacinth
Is more to me than platitudes
Rethundering from groin and plinth.

And at the first clear, careless strain
Poured from a woodbird's silver throat,
I have forgotten all the lore
The preacher bade me get by rote.

Beyond the shadow of the porch
I hear the wind among the trees,
The river babbling in the clove,
And that great sound that is the sea's,

Let me have brook and flower and bird
For counsellors, that I may learn
The very accent of their tongue,
And its least syllable discern.

For I, my brother, so would live
That I may keep the elder law
Of beauty and of certitude,
Of daring love and blameless awe.

Be others worthy to receive
The naked messages of God ;
I am content to find their trace
Among the people of the sod.

The gold-voiced dwellers of the wood
Flute up the morning as I pass;
And in the dusk I lay me down
With star-eyed children of the grass.

I harken for the winds of spring,
And haunt the marge of swamp and stream,
Till in the April night I hear
The revelation of the dream.

I listen when the orioles
Come up the earth with early June,
And the old apple-orchards spread
Their odorous glories to the moon.

So I would keep my natural days,
By sunlit sea, by moonlit hill,
With the dark beauty of the earth
Enchanted and enraptured still.

When all my lessons have been learned,
And the last year at school is done,
I shall put up my books and games;
" Good-by, my fellows, every one!"

The dusty road will not seem long,
Nor twilight lonely, nor forlorn
The everlasting whippoorwills
That lead me back where I was born.

And there beside the open door,
In a large country dim and cool,
Her waiting smile shall hear at last,
"Mother, I am come home from school."

Bliss Carman - An Appreciation

How many Canadians—how many even among the few who seek to keep themselves informed of the best in contemporary literature, who are ever on the alert for the new voices—realise, or even suspect, that this Northern land of theirs has produced a poet of whom it may be affirmed with confidence and assurance that he is of the great succession of English poets? Yet such—strange and unbelievable though it may seem—is in very truth the case, that poet being (to give him his full name) William Bliss Carman. Canada has full right to be proud of her poets, a small body though they are; but not only does Mr. Carman stand high and clear above them all—his place (and time cannot but confirm and justify the assertion) is among those men whose poetry is the shining glory of that great English literature which is our common heritage.

If any should ask why, if what has been just said is so, there has been—as must be admitted—no general recognition of the fact in the poet's home land, I would answer that there are various and plausible, if not good, reasons for it.

First of all, the poet, as thousands more of our young men of ambition and confidence have done, went early to the United States, and until recently, except for rare and brief visits to his old home down by the sea, has never returned to Canada—though for all that, I am able to state, on his own authority, he is still a Canadian citizen. Then all his books have had their original publication in the United States, and while a few of them have subsequently carried the imprints of Canadian publishers, none of these can be said ever to have made any special effort to push their sale. Another reason for the fact above mentioned is that Mr. Carman has always scorned to advertise himself, while his work has never been the subject of the log-rolling and booming which the work of many another poet has had—to his ultimate loss. A further reason is that he follows a rule of his own in preparing his books for publication. Most poets publish a volume of their work as soon as, through their industry and perseverance, they have material enough on hand to make publication desirable in their eyes. Not so with Mr. Carman, however, his rule being not to publish until he has done sufficient work of a certain general character or key to make a volume. As a result, you cannot fully know or estimate his work by one book, or two books, or even half a dozen; you must possess or be familiar with every one of the score and more volumes which contain his output of poetry before you can realise how great and how many-sided is his genius.

It is a common remark on the part of those who respond readily to the vigorous work of Kipling, or Masefield, even our own Service, that Bliss Carman's poetry has no relation to or concern with ordinary, everyday life. One would suppose that most persons who cared for poetry at all turned to it as a relief from or counter to the burdens and vexations of the daily round; but in any event, the remark referred to seems to me to indicate either the most casual acquaintance with Mr. Carman's work, or a complete misunderstanding and misapprehension of the meaning of it. I grant that you will find little or nothing in it all to remind you of the grim realities and vexing social problems of this modern existence of ours; but to say or to suggest that these things do not exist for Mr. Carman is to say or to suggest something which is the reverse of true. The truth is, he is aware of them as only one with the sensitive organism of a poet can be; but he does not feel that he has a call or mission to remedy them, and still less to sing of them. He therefore leaves the immediate problems of the day to those who choose, or are led, to occupy themselves therewith, and turns resolutely away to dwell upon those things which for him possess infinitely greater importance.

"What are they?" one who knows Mr. Carman only as, say, a lyrist of spring or as a singer of the delights of vagabondia probably will ask in some wonder. Well, the things which concern him above all, I would answer, are first, and naturally, the beauty and wonder of this world of ours, and next the mystery of the earthly pilgrimage of the human soul out of eternity and back into it again.

The poems in the present volume—which, by the way, can boast the high honor of being the very first regular Canadian edition of his work—will be evidence ample and conclusive to every reader, I am sure, of the place which

The perennial enchanted
Lovely world and all its lore

occupy in the heart and soul of Bliss Carman, as well as of the magical power with which he is able to convey the deep and unfailing satisfaction and delight which they possess for him. They, however, represent his latest period (he has had three well-defined periods), comprising selections from three of his last published volumes: The Rough Rider, Echoes from Vagabondia, and April Airs, together with a number of new poems, and do not show, except here and there and by hints and flashes, how great is his preoccupation with the problem of man's existence—

—the hidden import
Of man's eternal plight.

This is manifest most in certain of his earlier books, for in these he turns and returns to the greatest of all the problems of man almost constantly, probing, with consummate and almost unrivalled use of the art of expression, for the secret which surely, he clearly feels, lies hidden somewhere, to be discovered if one could but pierce deeply enough. Pick up Behind the Arras, and as you turn over page after page you cannot but observe how incessantly the poet's mind—like the minds of his two great masters, Browning and Whitman—works at this problem. In "Behind the Arras," the title poem; "In the Wings," "The Crimson House," "The Lodger," "Beyond the Gamut," "The Juggler"—yes, in every poem in the book—he takes up and handles the strange thing we know as, or call, life, turning it now this way, now that, in an effort to find out its meaning and purpose. He comes but little nearer success in this than do most of the rest of men, of course; but the magical and ever-fresh beauty of his expression, the haunting melody of his lines, the variety of his images and figures and the depth and range of his thought, put his searchings and ponderings in a class by themselves.

Lengthy quotation from Mr. Carman's books is not permitted here, and I must guide myself accordingly, though with reluctance, because I believe that in a study such as this the subject should be allowed to speak for himself as much as possible. In "Behind the Arras" the poet describes the passage from life to death as

A cadence dying down unto its source
In music's course,

and goes on to speak of death as

—the broken rhythm of thought and man,
The sweep and span
Of memory and hope
About the orbit where they still must grope
For wider scope,

To be through thousand springs restored, renewed,
With love imbrued,
With increments of will
Made strong, perceiving unattainment still
From each new skill.

Now follow some verses from "Behind the Gamut," to my mind the poet's greatest single achievement;

As fine sand spread on a disc of silver,
At some chord which bids the motes combine,
Heeding the hidden and reverberant impulse,
Shifts and dances into curve and line,

The round earth, too, haply, like a dust-mote,
Was set whirling her assigned sure way,
Round this little orb of her ecliptic
To some harmony she must obey.

And what of man?

Linked to all his half-accomplished fellows,
Through unfrontiered provinces to range—
Man is but the morning dream of nature,
Roused to some wild cadence weird and strange.

Here, now, are some verses from "Pulvis et Umbra," which is to be found in Mr. Carman's first book, Low Tide on Grand Pré, and in which the poet addresses a moth which a storm has blown into his window:

For man walks the world with mourning
Down to death and leaves no trace,
With the dust upon his forehead,
And the shadow on his face.

Pillared dust and fleeing shadow
As the roadside wind goes by,
And the fourscore years that vanish
In the twinkling of an eye.

"Pillared dust and fleeing shadow." Where in all our English literature will one find the life history of man summed up more briefly and, at the same time, more beautifully, than in that wonderful line? Now follows a companion verse to those just quoted, taken from "Lord of My Heart's Elation," which stands in the forefront of From the Green Book of the Bards. It may be remarked here that while the poet recurs again and again to some favorite thought or idea, it is never in the same words. His expression is always new and fresh, showing how deep and true is his inspiration. Again it is man who is pictured:

A fleet and shadowy column
Of dust and mountain rain,
To walk the earth a moment
And be dissolved again.

But while Mr. Carman's speculations upon life's meaning and the mystery of the future cannot but appeal to the thoughtful-minded, it is as an interpreter of nature that he makes his widest appeal. Bliss Carman, I must say here, and emphatically, is no mere landscape-painter; he never, or scarcely ever, paints a picture of nature for its own sake. He goes beyond the outward aspect of things and interprets or translates for us with less keen senses as only a poet whose feeling for nature is of the deepest and profoundest, who has gone to her whole-heartedly and been taken close to her warm bosom, can do. Is this not evident from these verses from "The Great Return"—originally called "The Pagan's Prayer," and for some inscrutable reason to be found only in the limited Collected Poems, issued in two stately volumes in 1905.

When I have lifted up my heart to thee,
Thou hast ever hearkened and drawn near,
And bowed thy shining face close over me,
Till I could hear thee as the hill-flowers hear.

When I have cried to thee in lonely need,
Being but a child of thine bereft and wrung,
Then all the rivers in the hills gave heed;
And the great hill-winds in thy holy tongue—

That ancient incommunicable speech—
The April stars and autumn sunsets know—
Soothed me and calmed with solace beyond reach
Of human ken, mysterious and low.

Who can read or listen to those moving lines without feeling that Mr. Carman is in very truth a poet of nature—nay, Nature's own poet? But how could he be other when, in "The Breath of the Reed" (From the Green Book of the Bards), he makes the appeal?

Make me thy priest, O Mother,
And prophet of thy mood,
With all the forest wonder
Enraptured and imbued.

As becomes such a poet, and particularly a poet whose birth-month is April, Mr. Carman sings much of the early spring. Again and again he takes up his woodland pipe, and lo! Pan himself and all his train troop joyously before us. Yet the singer's notes for all his singing never become wearied or strident; his airs are ever new and fresh; his latest songs are no less spontaneous and winning than were his first, written how many years ago, while at the same time they have gained in beauty and melody. What heart will not stir to the vibrant music of his immortal "Spring Song," which was originally published in the first Songs from Vagabondia, and the opening verses of which follow?

Make me over, mother April,
When the sap begins to stir!
When thy flowery hand delivers
All the mountain-prisoned rivers,
And thy great heart beats and quivers
To revive the days that were,
Make me over, mother April,
When the sap begins to stir!

Take my dust and all my dreaming,
Count my heart-beats one by one,
Send them where the winters perish;
Then some golden noon recherish
And restore them in the sun,
Flower and scent and dust and dreaming,
With their heart-beats every one!

That poem is sufficient in itself to prove that Bliss Carman has full right and title to be called Spring's own lyrist, though it may be remarked here that not all his spring poems are so unfeignedly joyous. Many of them indeed, have a touch, or more than a touch, of wistfulness, for the poet knows well that sorrow lurks under all joy, deep and well hidden though it may be.

Mr. Carman sings equally finely, though perhaps not so frequently, of summer and the other seasons; but as he has other claims upon our attention, I shall forbear to labor the fact, particularly as the following collection demonstrates it sufficiently. One of those other claims is as a writer of sea poetry. Few poets, it may be said, have pictured the majesty and the mystery, the beauty and the terror of the sea, better than he. His Ballads of Lost Haven is a veritable treasure-house for those whose spirits find kinship in wide expanses of moving waters. One of the best known poems in this volume is "The Gravedigger," which opens thus:

Oh, the shambling sea is a sexton old,

And well his work is done.
With an equal grave for lord and knave,
He buries them every one.

Then hoy and rip, with a rolling hip,
He makes for the nearest shore;
And God, who sent him a thousand ship,
Will send him a thousand more;
But some he'll save for a bleaching grave,
And shoulder them in to shore—
Shoulder them in, shoulder them in,
Shoulder them in to shore.

In "The City of the Sea" (Last Songs from Vagabondia) Mr. Carman speaks of the seabells sounding

The eternal cadence of sea sorrow
For Man's lot and immemorial wrong—
The lost strains that haunt the human dwelling
With the ghost of song.

Elsewhere he speaks of

The great sea, mystic and musical.

And here from another poem is a striking picture:

... the old sea
Seems to whimper and deplore
Mourning like a childless crone
With her sorrow left alone—
The eternal human cry
To the heedless passer-by.

I have said above that Mr. Carman has had three distinct periods, and intimated that the poems in the following collection are of his third period. The first period may be said to be represented by the Low Tide and Behind the Arras volumes, while the second is displayed in the three volumes of Songs from Vagabondia, which he published in association with his friend Richard Hovey. Bliss Carman was from the first too original and individual a poet to be directly influenced by anyone else; but there can be no doubt that his friendship with Hovey helped to turn him from over-preoccupation with mysteries which, for all their greatness, are not for man to solve, to an intenser realisation of the beauty and loveliness of the world about him and of the joys of human fellowship. The result is seen in such poems as "Spring Song," quoted in part above, and his perhaps equally well-known "The Joys of the Road," which appeared in the same volume with that poem, and a few verses from which follow:

Now the joys of the road are chiefly these:
A crimson touch on the hardwood trees;

A vagrant's morning wide and blue,

In early fall, when the wind walks, too;

A shadowy highway cool and brown,
Alluring up and enticing down

From rippled waters and dappled swamp,
From purple glory to scarlet pomp;

The outward eye, the quiet will,
And the striding heart from hill to hill.

Some of the finest of arman's work is contained in his elegiac or memorial poems, in which he commemorates Keats, Shelley, William Blake, Lincoln, Stevenson, and other men for whom he has a kindred feeling, and also friends whom he has loved and lost. Listen to these moving lines from "Non Omnis Moriar," written in memory of Gleeson White, and to be found in Last Songs from Vagabondia:

There is a part of me that knows,
Beneath incertitude and fear,
I shall not perish when I pass
Beyond mortality's frontier;

But greatly having joyed and grieved,
Greatly content, shall hear the sigh
Of the strange wind across the lone
Bright lands of taciturnity.

In patience therefore I await
My friend's unchanged benign regard,—
Some April when I too shall be
Spilt water from a broken shard.

In "The White Gull," written for the centenary of the birth of Shelley in 1892, and included in By the Aurelian Wall, he thus apostrophizes that clear and shining spirit:

O captain of the rebel host,
Lead forth and far!
Thy toiling troopers of the night
Press on the unavailing fight;
The sombre field is not yet lost,
With thee for star.

Thy lips have set the hail and haste
Of clarions free
To bugle down the wintry verge
Of time forever, where the surge
Thunders and trembles on a waste
And open sea.

In "A Seamark," a threnody for Robert Louis Stevenson, which appears in the same volume, the poet hails "R.L.S." (of whose tribe he may be said to be truly one) as

The master of the roving kind,

and goes on:

O all you hearts about the world
In whom the truant gypsy blood,
Under the frost of this pale time,
Sleeps like the daring sap and flood
That dreams of April and reprieve!
You whom the haunted vision drives,
Incredulous of home and ease.
Perfection's lovers all your lives!

You whom the wander-spirit loves
To lead by some forgotten clue
Forever vanishing beyond
Horizon brinks forever new;
Our restless loved adventurer,
On secret orders come to him,
Has slipped his cable, cleared the reef,
And melted on the white sea-rim.

"Perfection's lovers all your lives." Of these, it may be said without qualification, is Bliss Carman himself.

No summary of Mr. Carman's work, however cursory, would be worthy of the name if it omitted mention of his ventures in the realm of Greek myth. From the Book of Myths is made up of work of that sort, every poem in it being full of the beauty of phrase and melody of which Mr. Carman alone has the secret. The finest poems in the book, barring the opening one, "Overlord," are "Daphne," "The Dead Faun," "Hylas," and "At Phædra's Tomb," but I can do no more here than name them, for extracts would fail to reveal their full beauty. And beauty, after all is said, is the first and last thing with Mr. Carman. As he says himself somewhere:

The joy of the hand that hews for beauty
Is the dearest solace under the sun.

And again

The eternal slaves of beauty
Are the masters of the world.

A slave—a happy, willing slave—to beauty is the poet himself, and the world can never repay him for the message of beauty which he has brought it.

Kindred to From the Book of Myths, but much more important, is Sappho: One Hundred Lyrics, one of the most successful of the numerous attempts which have been made to recapture the poems by that high priestess of song which remain to us only in fragments. Mr. Carman, as Charles G. D. Roberts points out in an introduction to the volume, has made no attempt here at translation or paraphrasing; his venture has been "the most perilous and most alluring in the whole field of poetry"—that of imaginative and, at the same time, interpretive construction. Brief quotation again would fail to convey an adequate idea of the exquisiteness of the work, and all I can do, therefore, is to urge all lovers of real poetry to possess themselves of Sappho: One Hundred Lyrics, for it is literally a storehouse of lyric beauty.

I must not fail here to speak of From the Book of Valentines, which contains some lovely things, notably "At the Great Release." This is not only one of the finest of all Mr. Carman's poems, but it is also one of the finest poems of our time. It is a love poem, and no one possessing any real feeling for poetry can read it without experiencing that strange thrill of the spirit which only the highest form of poetry can communicate. "Morning and Evening," "In an Iris Meadow," and "A letter from Lesbos" must be also mentioned. In the last named poem, Sappho is represented as writing to Gorgo, and expresses herself in these moving words:

If the high gods in that triumphant time
Have calendared no day for thee to come
Light-hearted to this doorway as of old,
Unmoved I shall behold their pomps go by—
The painted seasons in their pageantry,
The silvery progressions of the moon,
And all their infinite ardors unsubdued,
Pass with the wind replenishing the earth

Incredulous forever I must live
And, once thy lover, without joy behold,
The gradual uncounted years go by,
Sharing the bitterness of all things made.

Mention must be now made of Songs of the Sea Children, which can be described only as a collection of the sweetest and tenderest love lyrics written in our time—

—the lyric songs
The earthborn children sing,
When wild-wood laughter throngs
The shy bird-throats of spring;
When there's not a joy of the heart
But flies like a flag unfurled,
And the swelling buds bring back
The April of the world.

So perfect and complete are these lyrics that it would be almost sacrilege to quote any of them unless entire. Listen however, to these verses:

The day is lost without thee,
The night has not a star.
Thy going is an empty room

Whose door is left ajar.

Depart: it is the footfall
Of twilight on the hills.
Return: and every rood of ground
Breaks into daffodils.

There are those who will have it that Bliss Carman has been away from Canada so long that he has ceased to be, in a real sense, a Canadian. Such assume rather than know, for a very little study of his work would show them that it is shot through and through with the poet's feeling for the land of his birth. Memories of his childhood and youthful years down by the sea are still fresh in Mr. Carman's mind, and inspire him again and again in his writing. "A Remembrance," at the beginning of the present collection, may be pointed to as a striking instance of this, but proof positive is the volume, Songs from a Northern Garden, for it could have been written only by a Canadian, born and bred, one whose heart and soul thrill to the thought of Canada. I would single out from this volume for special mention as being "Canadian" in the fullest sense "In a Grand Pré Garden," "The Keeper's Silence," "At Home and Abroad," "Killoleet," and "Above the Gaspereau," but have no space to quote from them.

But Mr. Carman is not only a Canadian, he is also a Briton; and evidence of this is his Ode on the Coronation, written on the occasion of the crowning of King Edward VII in 1902. This poem—the very existence of which is hardly known among us—ought to be put in the hands of every child and youth who speaks the English tongue, for no other, I dare maintain—nothing by Kipling, or Newbolt, or any other of our so-called "Imperial singers"—expresses more truly and more movingly the deep feeling of love and reverence which the very thought of England evokes in every son of hers, even though it may never have been his to see her white cliffs rise or to tread her storied ground:

O England, little mother by the sleepless Northern tide,
Having bred so many nations to devotion, trust, and pride,
Very tenderly we turn
With welling hearts that yearn
Still to love you and defend you,—let the sons of men discern
Wherein your right and title, might and majesty, reside.

In concluding this, I greatly fear, lamentably inadequate study, I come to the collection which follows, and which, as intimated above, represents the work of Mr. Carman's latest period. I must say at once that, while I yield to no one in admiration for Low Tide and the other books of that period, or for the work of the second period, as represented by the Songs from Vagabondia volumes, I have no hesitation in declaring that I regard the poet's work of the past few years with even higher admiration. It may not possess the force and vigor of the work which preceded it; but anything seemingly missing in that respect is more than made up for me by increased beauty and clarity of expression. The mysticism—verging, or more than verging, at times on symbolism—which marked his earlier poems, and which hung, as it were, as a veil between them and the reader, has gone, and the poet's thought or theme now lies clearly before us as in a mirror. What—to take a verse from the following pages at random—could be more pellucid, more crystal clear in expression—what indeed, could come closer to that achieving of the impossible at which every real poet must aim—than this from "In Gold Lacquer".

Gold are the great trees overhead,
And gold the leaf-strewn grass,

As though a cloth of gold were spread
To let a seraph pass.
And where the pageant should go by,
Meadow and wood and stream,
The world is all of lacquered gold,
Expectant as a dream.

The poet, happily, has fully recovered from the serious illness which laid him low some two years ago, and which for a time caused his friends and admirers the gravest concern, and so we may look forward hopefully to seeing further volumes of verse come from the press to make certain his name and fame. But if, for any reason, this should not be—which the gods forfend!—Later Poems, I dare affirm, must and will be regarded as the fine flower and crowning achievement of the genius and art of Bliss Carman.

R. H. HATHAWAY.
Toronto, 1921.

Bliss Carman – A Short Biography

William Bliss Carman was born in Fredericton, in New Brunswick on April 15th 1861. 'Bliss' was his mother's maiden name. She was descended from Daniel Bliss of Concord, Massachusetts, who was the great-grandfather to Ralph Waldo Emerson.

Carman was educated at Fredericton Collegiate School. Here, under the influence of the headmaster George Robert Parkin, he gained an appreciation of classical literature and was introduced to the poetry of many of the Pre-Raphaelites especially Dante Gabriel Rossetti and Algernon Charles Swinburne.

From here he graduated to the University of New Brunswick, obtaining his B.A. there in 1881. As is common with so many writers his first published piece was for the University magazine and for Carman that was in 1879.

England now beckoned and he spent a year at Oxford and then the University of Edinburgh (1882–1883). He returned home to Canada to work on his M.A. which he obtained from the University of New Brunswick in 1884.

Tragically his father died in January, 1885, followed by his mother in February of the following year. Carman now enrolled in Harvard University for a year. There he met and was part of a literary circle that included the American poet Richard Hovey, who would become his close friend, and later collaborator, on the successful Vagabondia poetry series. Carman and Hovey were members of the "Visionists" circle along with Herbert Copeland and F. Holland Day, who would later form the Boston publishing firm Copeland & Day and, in turn, launch Vagabondia.

After Harvard Carman briefly returned to Canada, but was back in Boston by February of 1890 saying "Boston is one of the few places where my critical education and tastes could be of any use to me in earning money. New York and London are about the only other places." However, he was unable to find work in Boston but was more successful in New York becoming the literary editor of the semi-religious New York Independent. There he helped Canadian poets get published and introduced them to a wider readership than they could receive in Canada.

However, Carman and work as an editor were not destined for a long career together and he was dismissed in 1892. There followed short stays with Current Literature, Cosmopolitan, The Chap-Book, and The Atlantic Monthly. Whilst these appointments provided the basis for a career and an income he was not suited to their demands. From 1895 he would only work as a contributor to magazines and newspapers whilst he worked on his volumes of poetry.

Carman first published a book of poetry in 1893 with Low Tide on Grand Pré. He had written the title poem in the summer of 1886 and it had (whilst he was still at Harvard) been published in the spring of 1887 by Atlantic Monthly. Despite its critical acceptance there was no Canadian company prepared to publish the volume. When an American company did so it went bankrupt. Life was becoming difficult for the young poet.

The following year was decidedly better. His partnership with Richard Hovey had given birth to Songs of Vagabondia and it was published by their friends at Copeland & Day. It was an immediate success. The young men were delighted at such a reception. It quickly sold out and was re-printed a number of times. Although these re-prints were small (usually 500-1000 copies) they were frequent.

On the back of this success they would write a further three volumes, which in their turn were almost as successful. They quickly became the center of a cult following, especially among students who empathized with the poetry's anti-materialistic themes, its celebration of personal freedom, and its glorification of comradeship."

The success of Songs of Vagabondia prompted the Boston firm, Stone & Kimball, to reissue Low Tide on Grand Pré and to hire Carman as the editor of its literary journal, The Chapbook. This ceased after a year when the company relocated and Carman expressed his desire to remain in Boston.

In 1885 Carman brought out Behind the Arras, a somewhat more serious and philosophical work centered on the premise of a long meditation using the speaker's house and its many rooms as a symbol of life and the choices to be made. However, the idea and its execution did not quite meld.

Signficantly, in 1896, Carman met Mrs Mary Perry King, who rapidly became patron, adviser and sometime lover. She put money in his pocket, and food in his mouth and, when he struck bottom, often repaired his confidence as well as helping to sell the work. She also later became his writing collaborator on two verse dramas.

Mitchell Kennerley, Carman's roommate wrote that, "On the rare occasions they had intimate relations they always advised me of by leaving a bunch of violets — Mary favorite flower — on the pillow of my bed." If her husband, Dr. King, knew of this arrangement he seems not to have objected. He was a great supporter of Carman's career and seemingly his wife's complicated involvement with that.

In 1897 Carman published Ballad of Lost Haven, a collection of poetry about the sea. Its notable poems include the macabre sea shanty, The Gravedigger. The following year, 1898, came By the Aurelian Wall, the title poem itself was an elegy to John Keats and the book a collection of formal elegies.

In 1899 his publisher, Lamson, Wolffe was taken over by the Boston firm of Small, Maynard & Co., who had also acquired the rights to Low Tide on Grand Pré. The copyrights to of his books were now held by one publisher and, in lieu of earnings, Carman took what would ultimately be a disastrous financial stake in the company.

As the century turned Carman was hard at work on what would eventually be a five-volume set of poetry; "Pans Pipes". Pan, the goat-god, was traditionally associated with poetry and the coming together of the earthly and the divine. The five volumes were all published between 1902 – 1905.

The inspiration for this came from Mary who had persuaded Carman to write in both prose and poetry about the ideas of 'unitrinianism.' This drew on the theories of François-Alexandre-Nicolas-Chéri Delsarte and was defined as a strategy of mind-body-spirit harmonization aimed at undoing the physical, psychological, and spiritual damage caused by urban modernity. The definition may be rather woolly but for Carman it resulted in some very fine work across the five-volume series. This shared belief between Mary and Carman created a further bond but did isolate him from his circle of friends.

The excellence of a number of these poems did much to install Carman as the most noted of Canadian Poets and eventually their own Poet Laureate. Among the most often quoted and printed are "The Dead Faun" (from Volume I), "Lord of My Heart's Elation" (Volume II) and many of the erotic poems from Volume III.

In the middle of publication in 1903, Small, Maynard failed and with it went all the assets Carman had tied up in the company.

Carman immediately signed with another Boston publisher, L.C. Page, who would publish seven new books of Carman poetry in this hectic period up to 1905. They released a further three books based on Carman's Transcript columns, and a prose work on Unitrinianism, The Making of Personality, that he'd written with Mary King.

Carman now felt secure enough to pursue his 'dream project,' namely a deluxe edition of his collected poetry to 1903. Page acquired the distribution rights on the condition that the book be sold privately, by subscription. Unfortunately, the demand wasn't there and it failed. Carman was deeply disappointed and lost faith in Page. However, their grip on his copyrights was absolute and sadly no further collected editions were to be published during his lifetime.

By 1904 his income was restricted and the offer to be editor-in-chief of the 10-volume project, The World's Best Poetry, was eagerly accepted.

For Carman perhaps his best years as a poet were now behind him. From 1908 he lived near the Kings' New Canaan, Connecticut, estate, that he named "Sunshine", or in the summer in a cabin in the Catskills, which he called "Moonshine."

With Literary tastes now moving away from what he could provide his income further dwindled and his health started to deteriorate.

In 1912 Carman published the final work in the Vagabondia series. Richard Hovey had died in 1900 and so this last work was purely his. It has a distinct elegiac tone as if remembering the past works themselves.

Although Carman was not politically active he did campaign during the World War One, as a member of the Vigilantes, who supported the American entry into the titanic struggle on the Allied side.

By 1920, Carman was impoverished and recovering from a near-fatal attack of tuberculosis. He returned to Canada and began to undertake a series of publicly successful and somewhat lucrative reading tours, saying "there is nothing worth talking of in book sales compared with reading. Breathless attention, crowded halls, and a strange, profound enthusiasm such as I never guessed could be,' he reported to a friend. 'And good thrifty money too. Think of it! An entirely new life for me, and I am the most surprised person in Canada.'"

On October 28th, 1921 Carman was honored at a dinner held by the newly-formed Canadian Authors' Association, at the Ritz Carlton Hotel in Montreal, where he was crowned Canada's Poet Laureate with a wreath of maple leaves.

Carman is placed among the Confederation Poets, a group that included his cousin, Charles G.D. Roberts, Archibald Lampman, and Duncan Campbell Scott. Carman was perhaps the best and is credited with the widest recognition. However, whilst the others carefully supplemented their income with writing novels and works for the magazines, or even other careers, Carman only wrote poetry together with a small amount of writing on literary ideas, philosophy, and aesthetics.

He continued his reading tours, and by 1925 had finally secured a new Canadian publisher; McClelland & Stewart (Toronto), who issued a collection of selected earlier verse and would now became his main publisher. Although they benefited from Carman's increased popularity and his revered position in Canadian literature, his former publisher L.C. Page would not relinquish its copyrights to his earlier works.

In his last years, Carman was a member of the Halifax literary and social set, The Song Fishermen and in 1927 he edited The Oxford Book of American Verse.

William Bliss Carman died of a brain hemorrhage, at the age of 68, in New Canaan on the 8th June, 1929. He was cremated in New Canaan and his ashes interred at Forest Hill Cemetery, Fredericton, with a national memorial service held at the Anglican cathedral there.

It was only a quarter of a century later, on May 13th, 1954, that a scarlet maple tree was planted at his graveside, to honour his request in the 1892 poem "The Grave-Tree":

Let me have a scarlet maple
For the grave-tree at my head,
With the quiet sun behind it,
In the years when I am dead.

Bliss Carman – A Concise Bibliography

Poetry Collections
Low Tide on Grand Pre: A Book of Lyrics (1893)
Songs from Vagabondia (1894)

A Seamark: A Threnody for Robert Louis Stevenson (1895)
Behind the Arras: A Book of the Unseen (1895)
More Songs from Vagabondia (1896)
Ballads of Lost Haven: A Book of the Sea (1897)
By the Aurelian Wall: And Other Elegies (1898)
A Winter Holiday (1899)
Last Songs from Vagabondia (1901)
Ballads and Lyrics (1902)
Ode on the Coronation of King Edward (1902)
Pipes of Pan: From the Book of Myths (1902)
Pipes of Pan: From the Green Book of the Bards (1903)
Pipes of Pan: Songs of the Sea Children (1904)
Pipes of Pan: Songs from a Northern Garden (1904)
Pipes of Pan: From the Book of Valentines (1905)
Sappho: One Hundred Lyrics (1904)
Poems (1905)
The Rough Rider: And Other Poems (1909)
A Painter's Holiday, and Other Poems (1911)
Echoes from Vagabondia (1912)
April Airs: A Book of New England Lyrics (1916)
The Man of The Marne: And Other Poems (1918)
The Vengeance of Noel Brassard: A Tale of the Acadian Expulsion (1919)
Far Horizons (1925)
Later Poems (1926)
Sanctuary: Sunshine House Sonnets (1929)
Wild Garden (1929)
Bliss Carman's Poems (1931)

Drama
Bliss Carman & Mary Perry King. Daughters of Dawn: A Lyrical Pageant of a Series of Historical Scenes for Presentation with Music and Dancing (1913)
Bliss Carman & Mary Perry King. Earth Deities: And Other Rhythmic Masques (1914)

Prose Collections
The Kinship of Nature (1904)
The Poetry of Life (1905)
The Friendship of Art (1908)
The Making of Personality (1908)
Talks on Poetry and Life; Being a Series of Five Lectures Delivered Before the University of Toronto, December 1925 (Speech). transcribed by Blanche Hume. 1926.
Bliss Carman's Scrap-Book: A Table of Contents (Pierce, Lorne, editor) (1931)

Editor
The World's Best Poetry (10 volumes) (1904)
The Oxford Book of American Verse (U.S. editor) (1927)

Carman, Bliss; Pierce, Lorne, editors (1935). Our Canadian Literature: Representative Verse, English and French.

www.ingramcontent.com/pod-product-compliance
Lightning Source LLC
Chambersburg PA
CBHW060049050426
42448CB00011B/2363